OBSERVE, THINK, TRY!

by F. Isabel Campoy
illustrated by Roberta Ludlow

Inventions are created to solve problems large and small. Some inventions are very simple, but it took a creative person to come up with each one.

Think of the invention BRAKES. All of these things have brakes.

cars	trains	bicycles
strollers	trucks	tractors
motorcycles	wheelchairs	buses
roller skates	ambulances	fire trucks

Brakes were invented to solve a problem. What problem do they solve? Think of how you would put brakes on one of these things.

skateboard   shopping cart   ice skate

4

Observe the way brakes work on a bicycle. Think about how brakes could work on a shopping cart or something else that moves. Draw a picture of your invention. Then make a model of it and try it out! Observe, think, try!

Think of the invention SHOES. There are many different kinds of shoes. Why do you think each of these kinds of shoes was invented?

**sneakers   hiking boots   ballet slippers
moccasins   snow boots   sandals**

Observe the different ways shoes are made to meet different needs. Think of an activity for which you would need special shoes. Draw the shoes you would invent. Then try out your idea by making a model. Observe, think, try!

Many things that were invented long ago are still used today. The lightbulb was invented by Thomas Edison. He was an inventor who observed a problem. People had always used candles or torches for light. Edison wanted to use electricity instead.

Edison thought of a way to solve the problem. Then he tried out his invention. He had to try many times to get it right. He did not give up. He continued to observe, think, and try!

When you travel to a new place, you may find some things different there. You may not know how to deal with them. How can you solve this problem?

Think of the things that were new to you when you arrived at your new school. Make a list like this one.

language	**clothing**
school rules	**games**
food	**books**
flag	**songs**

How can you get along in a new place? Observe, think, try!

First, observe the people around you. Watch what they do and how they do it. Observe when and why they do it.

Next, think about how you can do it. Then try to do it yourself. You will make some mistakes, but don't give up. Observe, think, try!

Look back at the list on page 10. Think about the word *language,* for example. It can be difficult for new students to understand what others are saying. How could they solve this problem?

One way to solve this problem is to look for words that are like words in your first language. Observe these words from the paragraph above.

list	**difficult**
page	**students**
language	**example**

Do some of these words look like words in your language? Think about what these words mean. Then try translating the paragraph into your language.

Look again at the list on page 10. This time, think about school rules. Make a list of the rules you have observed in your new school. Share your list with a friend. Talk about the school rules you have both observed. Try to learn the rules. You may make some mistakes, but don't give up. Observe, think, try!

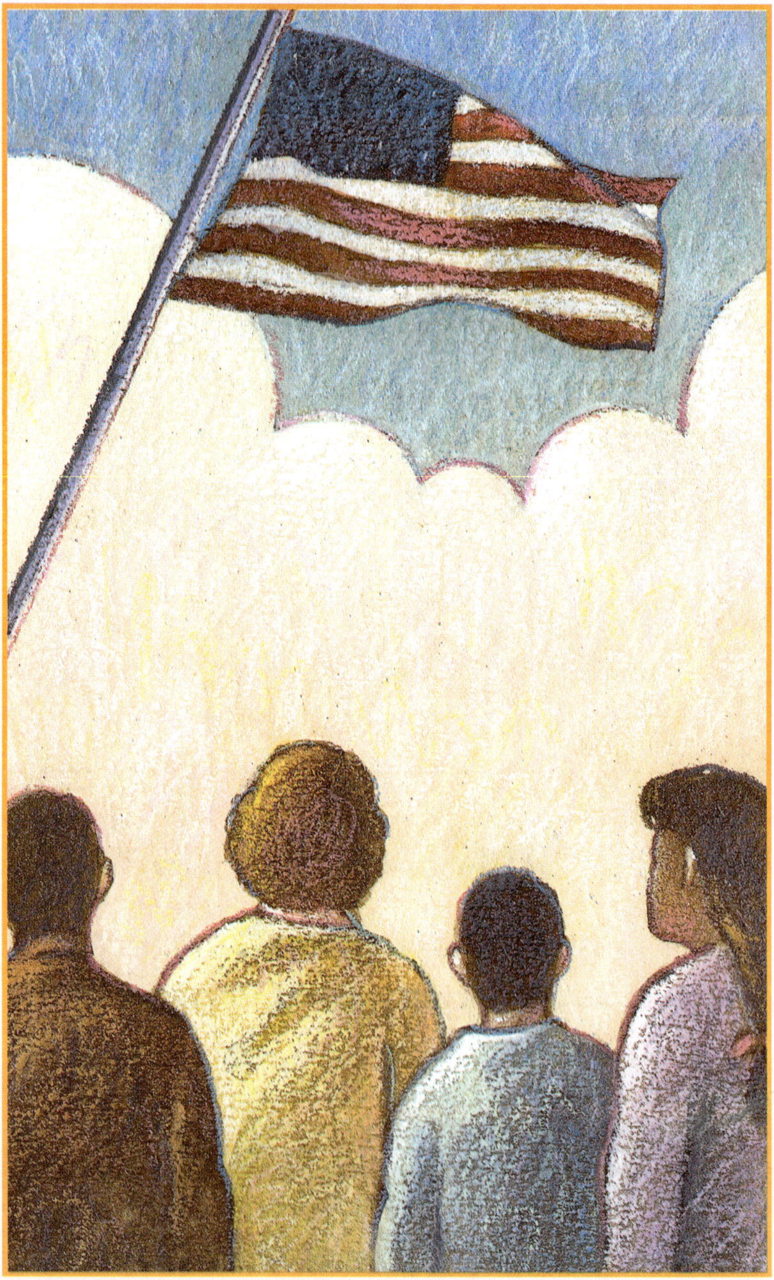

Have you moved from another country to the United States? So have many other people. They moved here to find good things. They also brought with them good things to share.

Observe your school and your neighborhood. What good things do you find? Make a list of the things you think are good about your school and your neighborhood.

Now think about something in your school or your neighborhood that is a problem. How could you solve this problem? Observe the problem. Think of a way to solve it. Then try your idea. Work with your friends, family, and neighbors. Don't give up. Observe, think, try!

You can always think of new ways to solve problems. Inventors make things better and easier for many people. You can invent something to make things easier for you!

When you observe a problem, think of some ways to solve it. Then try out your ideas. Observe, think, try!